I0843354

Ornamental Cacti

The Culture and Decorative Value of the Cactus

by United States Dept. of Agriculture

with an introduction by Roger Chambers

This work contains material that was originally published in 1912.

This publication was created and published for the public benefit, utilizing public funding and is within the Public Domain.

This edition is reprinted for educational purposes and in accordance with all applicable Federal Laws.

Introduction Copyright 2018 by Roger Chambers

Self Reliance Books

Get more historic titles on animal and stock breeding, gardening and old fashioned skills by visiting us at:

http://selfreliancebooks.blogspot.com/

Introduction

I am pleased to present yet another title on Ginseng.

The work is in the Public Domain and is re-printed here in accordance with Federal Laws.

As with all reprinted books of this age that are intended to perfectly reproduce the original edition, considerable pains and effort had to be undertaken to correct fading and sometimes outright damage to existing proofs of this title. At times, this task is quite monumental, requiring an almost total "rebuilding" of some pages from digital proofs of multiple copies. Despite this, imperfections still sometimes exist in the final proof and may detract from the visual appearance of the text.

I hope you enjoy reading this book as much as I enjoyed making it available to readers again.

Roger Chambers

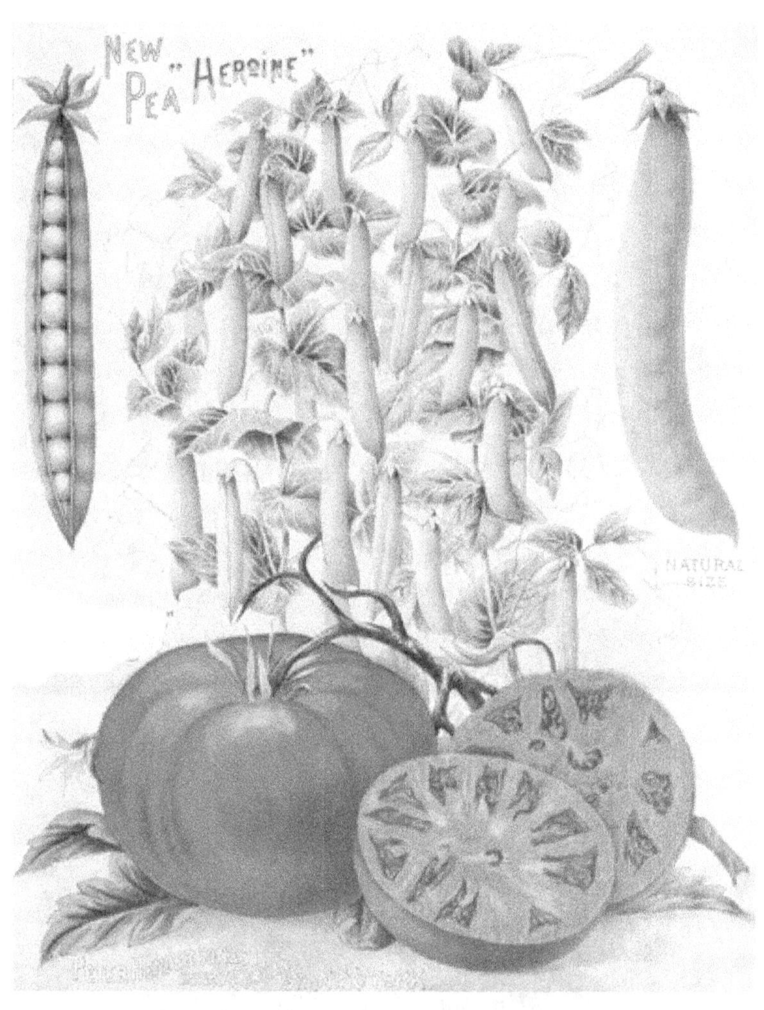

NEW
PEA "HEROINE"
NATURAL SIZE

LETTER OF TRANSMITTAL.

U. S. Department of Agriculture,
Bureau of Plant Industry,
Office of the Chief,
Washington, D. C., July 9, 1912.

Sir: I transmit herewith and recommend for publication as Bulletin No. 262 of this Bureau an illustrated manuscript entitled "Ornamental Cacti: Their Culture and Decorative Value." This manuscript was prepared by Mr. Charles Henry Thompson, who carried on the investigations under the direction of the Agriculturist in Charge of Cactus Investigations in the Office of Farm Management. Owing to its strictly horticultural nature, it was deemed wise that it be issued from the Office of Horticultural Investigations and Arlington Farm.

Mr. Thompson has long been in charge of the Succulent Collections of the Missouri Botanical Garden, St. Louis. His position and experience eminently qualify him to discuss this subject.

It is believed that while this bulletin may be of interest to cactus fanciers throughout the country, its particular field of usefulness will prove to be the warmer and drier southwestern regions where these plants are extensively used for decorative gardening.

Respectfully,

B. T. Galloway,
Chief of Bureau.

Hon. James Wilson,
    Secretary of Agriculture.

CONTENTS.

ILLUSTRATIONS.

B. P. I.—768.

ORNAMENTAL CACTI: THEIR CULTURE AND DECORATIVE VALUE.

INTRODUCTION.

With the exception of a few species of Rhipsalis the cacti are strictly indigenous to the Western Hemisphere. The introduction of these plants into Europe evidently began soon after the discovery of America. The English, Dutch, and Spanish traders, who early carried on a commercial business in the West Indies, South America, Central America, and Mexico, took back to their respective countries many interesting and curious plants then new to the gardens and plant lovers of Europe.

In the earliest published reports of the introduced and cultivated plants of European gardens we frequently find accounts and in many instances illustrations of cacti. Gradually additional plants were introduced, until at the time Linnæus published his Species Plantarum (1753) he recognized 22 species, all of which he included under the generic name of Cactus. They were commonly known as thistles, probably from the spiny character of their protective armor. The smaller, more or less globose forms, were called "melon" thistles, while the taller ones were called "torch" thistles or "candle" thistles. The *Ficus indica,* or Indian fig, and several other species of Opuntia were introduced into the Mediterranean region at a very early date.

From the time of the publication by Linnæus the steady introduction of new plants was continued from the Western Hemisphere into Europe. These importations included many forms of cacti. Miller, in his dictionary, enumerates a number of species distinct from those recognized by Linnæus. Others were described and published from time to time by Haworth, Link and Otto, Salm-Dyck, P. De Candolle, Lemaire, Pfeiffer, and others. The most extensive modern systematic work is Gesammtbeschreibung der Kakteen, by Dr. Karl Schumann.

It was not until within the past half century that any special interest in cacti was manifested in America. A few species, such as the night-blooming cereus (*Cereus grandiflorus* and *Cereus nycticalus*), queen of the night (*Phyllocactus acuminatus*), crab cactus (*Epiphyllum truncatum*), and the rat-tail cactus (*Cereus flagelliformis*), had become favorites as house plants. General collections of this group of the plant world by Dr. George Engelmann laid the foundation for the large collection at the Missouri Botanical Garden at St. Louis, Mo. Similar interest manifested by Dr. Asa Gray added materially to the collection at the Botanical Garden at Cambridge, Mass. As the public became more acquainted with these bizarre forms of vegetation, a livelier interest in them sprang up, and many persons throughout the country began to gather private collections. Fanciers became so numerous that in certain localities clubs or societies were organized among them, where ideas and experiences as to the culture of these plants could be discussed and specimens exchanged. Experience was the high-priced teacher from whom these collectors had to gain their knowledge. Similar organizations were formed in Germany, where amateur collectors were numerous, and also in France and in England. Many articles have been published in the horticultural journals of these countries describing proper methods of propagation and culture, and Mr. Watson, of the Kew Gardens, England, issued a Handbook of Cactus Culture. These helps have disseminated a better general knowledge of methods to be employed, but the soil and climatic conditions of Europe differ so materially from those of various parts of America that their rules are not well adapted to our own special needs.

The growing interest in this group of plants in America and the inadaptability of rules for general gardening in growing them, as well as of rules laid down for their special care by European growers, have created a demand in this country for a work that will include both general and special rules that may be applied to any part of our country. To meet this demand is the writer's purpose in putting forth this bulletin. Naturally, much of the material herein contained is compiled from the experiences of others, but use of it is made only in so far as it agrees with the writer's experience and observations, gained during the years spent in caring for the collection at the Missouri Botanical Garden and in traveling through the native haunts of these plants throughout the Southwestern States and in Mexico, as well as in the examination of many private collections.

PROPAGATION OF CACTI FROM SEEDS.

Most cacti yield seeds abundantly. Ordinarily, few of these seeds germinate and develop into mature plants, because of unfavorable environment. The seeds are usually fertile, however, and when planted under proper conditions a large percentage of them will germinate and with a little care will produce plants in abundance.

The best soil for growing cacti from seed has proved to be a thoroughly decomposed sod mixed with at least its own volume of sand. After these ingredients have been carefully mixed, they are run through a sieve of about ¼-inch mesh, which removes any large particles and all superfluous root fibers, making a loose soil which drains very readily. It is not necessary that the soil be very rich in humus, and manured soils should always be avoided because of their undue tendency to hold moisture. They are also a medium for producing germs of decay. An open, drainable soil is the chief requisite for cultivating cacti.

For germinating the seeds an ordinary 4-inch pot is very convenient. New pots are preferable, but old pots may be used with safety if thoroughly sterilized. Porous pots are soon covered with green algæ when left in a moist place for any considerable time. This growth will spread over the surface of the soil in a close blanket which precludes the free access of air and seriously retards the drainage of superfluous water. These algæ will in time grow over the little seedlings that have survived other adverse conditions and will smother them to death. To combat the algæ the pots should be thoroughly sterilized just previous to being used, and to accomplish this object two efficient methods have been found. One method is to bake or burn the pots, so that all life on them or in their pores may be destroyed. The other method is to soak the pots for a time in a weak solution of copper sulphate and then thoroughly wash them in the same solution. If a very strong solution of the copper sulphate is used, some of it will be left in the pores of the clay, and later, when the seedlings are being watered, enough may pass through the soil to injure the tender young plants.

Reasonable care should be exercised in preparing the pot for planting. As a rule the drain hole in the bottom of the pot is too small and is easily clogged. This hole should be enlarged, as thorough drainage must be maintained in growing cacti. The pot should be filled to one-fourth its depth with small bits of broken pots, and on these the prepared soil should be placed and pressed or shaken together firmly but not packed hard. The soil surface is then leveled by the use of a round, flat-faced tamper of a diameter to just fill the pot. The soil should not be packed but should be lightly tamped, with only sufficient effort to produce a smooth, level surface. This surface should be about half an inch from the top of the pot. Over it the seeds are evenly distributed and then covered with a very thin layer of soil, upon which is spread a layer of fine gravel to a depth of about one-fourth of an inch. This layer of gravel is important in many ways. As the pots are later watered with a fine spray, it prevents the surface of the soil from washing and consequently keeps the seeds from being disarranged. It also promotes the free passage of moist air through the spaces between the bits of gravel, which, together with the shading by the gravel, prevents the surface of the soil from becoming dry and baked. It also checks the growth of algæ over the soil surface.

As the seedlings grow they easily force their way through the gravel to the sunlight. For the first few months of their existence, cactus seedlings are but small, globular, balloon-shaped or cylindrical bodies, composed of very thin-walled cells filled to turgidity with water. They are so tender and delicate that they readily "damp off" if subjected to a sudden change from a high to a low temperature. The death rate of seedlings from this cause has been greatly minimized or almost wholly checked by the use of the gravel over the surface of the soil. This layer, with its intervening spaces, acts as a protection from sudden changes in temperature during that period of their growth when the seedlings are most susceptible to injury. By the time they have grown sufficiently large to project beyond the gravel they have become hardier and more robust in structure. Again, the gravel layer is of great value in that it keeps the surface of the soil moist. The little seedlings have exceedingly fine and delicate roots which spread out near the surface of the soil. If this surface is allowed to dry out to the depth of one-eighth of an inch or more, these delicate rootlets will be destroyed and the seedlings will be damaged or killed. In most instances the diminutive plant has not enough food stored up in its body to keep it alive until another set of feeding roots can be produced, and it starves to death. For watering, a vessel should be used that gives a fine, gentle spray, in order to avoid the danger of washing the seeds from their position or of injuring the delicate young seedlings. Watering should be done at least once a day. The temperature of the propagating house or frame should be kept as nearly uniform as possible and should not vary much from 70° F.

The proper time for transplanting the seedlings differs for different genera and species, but they should usually be left in the germination pot until the plant shows at least three or four clusters of spines. By that time the tissues will have become considerably hardened and a very good root system will have been formed. The taller growing species, such as Cereus, will be the first ones ready for transplanting. Mamilláris and kindred genera and plants of similar growth will be the last. The seedlings should be transplanted into a flat sufficiently small for convenient handling, which should be provided with drainage openings in the bottom. It should be filled with the same kind of material and soil as used in the germination pots, the surface to be carefully leveled in the same way. The rows should be about an inch apart, with the same interval between seedlings in the row. After the flat has been filled with the seedlings a thin layer of clean gravel should be placed all over the soil surface and close up around the plants. The flats should then be placed in a perfectly level position, so that the soil will not shift from one side toward the other when watered. Cactus plants are of slow growth and may remain in the flat for several months before being potted. The proper time for potting is when the plants have grown so large that they begin to crowd each other or when the roots of adjacent plants begin to intermingle. In preparing pots for individual plants the same method should be followed as for the preparation of the germination pots, except that a coarse soil may be used to advantage. It is not advisable to begin with pots smaller than 2½ inches, as they dry out too rapidly.

VEGETATIVE PROPAGATION.

Almost all cacti may be readily propagated from cuttings. The plants are so soft in tissue and so filled with water that any bruise or mutilation is likely to be the point of attack of a rot fungus, which quickly destroys them; so, in making the cutting, a clean, sharp knife must be used and a smooth surface left on the cut end. The cutting should then be placed in a dry atmosphere for a day or more, until, by drying, a kind of cuticle has formed over the cut surface. The cutting may then be rooted in sand on a bench or planted directly in pots. In the warmer, drier regions it may be placed directly in the open ground, provided the soil has perfect drainage. In greenhouse culture it is best not to place much of the cutting below the surface of the soil or sand; 1 inch is sufficient for large plants, and less than that for smaller ones, in proportion to the size of the cutting. When the cutting is long and likely to fall over, a stick should be inserted in the soil by its side and the two securely tied together until roots have been formed. When mature plants are shipped in from the field the roots are always more or less injured. It is always best to cut away the roots, let the wounds dry and heal for a time, and then plant them as cuttings. Many of the opuntias are naturally adapted to propagate themselves vegetatively. The stems are readily detached at the joints. These stems fall to the ground and in a short time develop roots and begin to grow as independent plants. Some are adapted for even wider dissemination. The spines which they bear are very sharp and stiff, and are barbed. These spines penetrate the skins of passing animals and cling so tenaciously that the joints bearing them are readily detached from the parent plant and may be carried a considerable distance before being released from their carrier. Once lodged in proper soil under favorable climatic conditions, they soon become new individual plants. In many of the opuntias the fruits are sterile but proliferous. They may be removed and treated as cuttings and will readily produce new plants. Many of the smaller forms, such as Echinocactus, Echinocereus, and Mamillaria, produce branches (Pl. I) which are readily detachable and are easily rooted as cuttings. Some species of Mamillaria have side shoots which are so lightly attached that they break off by a slight touch. Such plants depend almost entirely on vegetative propagation and rarely produce flowers and fruit.

GRAFTING.

Grafting is easily accomplished throughout this whole group of plants. The possibilities of uniting both species and genera seem to be unlimited. For a long time it has been a practice to graft Epiphyllum on Peireskia or some upright, stiff-stemmed Cereus in order to produce a more decorative bush plant. The rat-tail cactus (*Cereus flagelliformis*) is frequently treated in the same manner. Aside from its ornamental possibilities, grafting may be resorted to profitably as a means of propagation. It not infrequently happens that a plant becomes decayed at its base, and when all evidence of decay or disease has been removed there will be so little healthy tissue left that it is next to impossible to get it to grow as a cutting. Such a piece may be grafted on a healthy stock and the plant be preserved, if the growing tip is intact. A cleft graft or a saddle graft is more desirable where either of these can be employed, since they require less work in preparation and give a good large surface for the union of the tissues. The mucilaginous sap that exudes from the cut surface of a cactus plant allows the stock and scion to slip apart very easily, and the parts become disarranged unless proper precaution is used to prevent it. For this purpose the needle-like spines of Peireskia or Opuntia may be used. The two parts are pressed firmly together into the desired position, and then a spine is thrust through the united portions, securely pinning them in that position. No wax is required, but it is best to closely wrap the graft with raffia to exclude the air. The grafted plants are then placed in a warm, moderately moist place until the tissues have become thoroughly knitted together. They should not be placed where they might be subject to drying, for under such conditions the cut surface will be the first to dry, and consequently a perfect union will be prevented.

With small globose or thick plants, such as Mamillaria (Pl. II), Echinocactus, Echinocereus, etc., a different method is preferable. The head of the plant is cut away with a perfectly smooth transverse cut. (Pl. III.) A stock is selected which has about the same diameter as the scion, and it is also given a smooth transverse cut. The two flat surfaces are then pressed firmly together and held in place by tying them together with a cotton or other soft cord. It is quite essential that clean instruments be used to prevent the inoculation of the plant with disease germs. A number of the upright-growing species of Cereus have been used successfully for stocks, and there seems to be no limit to the number of species that may be used. It has been found, however, that some are better than others for the purpose. When it is desired to have the scion a foot or more high, good stocks may be obtained from *Cereus stellatus, C. serpentinus*, and other species of similar habits of growth. These stocks are preferable for use in grafting *Cereus flagelliformis* and species of Epiphyllum and Rhipsalis, which normally grow in a pendent position. Where only short stocks are desired the above may be used, and also *Cereus nycticalus, C. tortuosus, C. bomplandii, C. macdonaldiae*, and *C. grandiflorus*. These latter plants are weak stemmed when allowed to grow tall; hence, they can not be used for high grafts unless supported by a stake of some kind. All these species are readily grown from cuttings, which should be somewhat longer than the stock is to be. When the cutting is thoroughly rooted it should be potted and kept in good growing condition until a new root system has formed. It will then be ready to receive the scion after having been cut back to the desired height.

CULTURE.

Cacti thrive from southern Canada to far down in South America. Between these extreme points there is scarcely any combination of atmospheric and soil conditions that does not support one or more species of the family. They are found near the seashore in the Tropics, as well as high up on the mountains, where in winter they are subjected to severe frosts. They are most abundant, however, in the higher semiarid tablelands. With these facts in mind, it is clear that when collected they can not all be treated alike, but must be grouped according to the conditions under which the individuals grow in their native haunts, and each group must receive a different treatment to accord therewith.

Epiphyllum, Rhipsalis, a few species of Phyllocactus, and some species of Cereus are epiphytic in their tropical homes and should be given like treatment in conservatories. They should be grown under practically the same warm, moist atmospheric conditions as are tropical orchids, which may be grown in baskets of peat and moss, or be trained on blocks or stumps, or on walls, wherever the roots have opportunity to penetrate a moisture-laden medium. Most species of Phyllocactus and of the climbing species of Cereus should be grown in orchidlike conditions of temperature and humidity but in very loose, moderately rich soil. For this purpose a mixture of loam, sand, and an abundance of thoroughly decomposed leaf mold makes an excellent soil. By far the greater number of species of cacti are terrestrial in their habits and are indigenous to warm, semi-arid regions. The annual rainfall in these regions is very slight and continues for only a brief period. It is difficult to reproduce such conditions in our northern climate, and it is found that cacti can best be grown here by minimizing the action of our abundant rains by having the plants placed in a thoroughly well-drained situation. It is equally difficult to reproduce the conditions in our conservatories, where they are heated artificially, because of the drying effect of the heat. This condition may be largely counteracted by a judicious watering of the soil about the plants. For this group of plants it is not necessary that the soil be very rich, but it is essential that it be very open and thoroughly drained.

In repotting older plants it is best to disturb the roots as little as possible. Enlarge the drain opening in the bottom of the pot and place over it broken pots or other coarse material to not less than 1 inch in depth, to insure perfect, uniform drainage. Over the coarse material put a layer of soil. Remove the plant to be repotted by inverting the pot and gently tapping its rim on the edge of a bench or some such solid structure. The whole body of dirt will come out in a lump. Remove any bits of broken pots that may be attached to the bottom, but leave the soil in place about the roots. The surface soil should be removed if it shows any evidence of containing algæ or fungous growths. Place this ball of dirt and roots in the next pot and pack fresh soil about it, leaving sufficient space at the top to receive water. In conservatories pots are apt to become coated with green algæ, and old pots especially so, because the spores of the algæ are likely to remain in the pores of a pot from its previous use. Old pots should be thoroughly sterilized, as heretofore explained for the germination pots. After the plant is potted the surface of the soil should be covered with fine gravel to a depth of at least half an inch.

The soil about the plants should never be allowed to become absolutely dry for any great length of time or the roots will be seriously injured; on the other hand, it must not be kept saturated, but should be kept moist at all times. Any superfluous water standing about the base of the plant or in the soil about its roots is a serious menace, since it acts as a medium through which germs of rot enter the plant and soon destroy it. Cactus plants contain so much liquid that decay works very rapidly through them. When decay is once started it is difficult to save the plant; hence, the urgent necessity for having thorough drainage below the plant and a thoroughly drainable soil. Failures in the growing of cacti are undoubtedly due more to the neglect of this precaution than to all other causes combined.

Cacti do not require to be pruned beyond the removal of dead portions and to keep the plants in shape within the space allotted to them. Pruning may be done at any time, but preferably when the atmosphere is dry, so that the cut surface may dry and heal quickly.

In conservatories during the colder season, in order that the air may be sufficiently dry, a temperature ranging from 60° to 70° F. should be maintained. A temperature lower than 60° for any considerable length of time would hold the moisture about the plants too long and invite decay. During the warmer season, if the plants are kept in the house it is necessary that it be kept fully ventilated. The aim is to have at all times a dry atmosphere and a moderately moist well-drained soil. If the plants are placed in open ground during the summer months and their pots plunged in the beds, these beds likewise must be thoroughly drained. In placing a collection out of doors as a permanent planting, a situation should be selected, if possible, where the ground slopes sufficiently to insure perfect drain-age. If natural drainage is impossible, a system of drain tiles should be placed throughout the area to be planted and the soil above the tiles should be made loose and porous by the abundant addition of gravel and sand. Out-of-door planting is preferably done during the dry season, so that the cut surfaces or any injured portions of the plants will dry over quickly and be less easily infected with rot.

DISEASES.

The one disease from which cacti suffer more than any other is rot. The plant body is so saturated with water that it forms an excellent medium for the growth of this disease. It is liable to attack the plant at any point where the germs have opportunity to reach the interior. Any cut or bruised place presents the most favorable point for infection, from which the disease rapidly spreads and destroys the plant. Water dripping on a plant for even a short time may induce infection. By far the greater number of plants receive the infection through their bases or roots, whence it works upward through the center of the plant. By the time it has reached the surface the plants are usually too far gone to be saved. If the disease is detected before it has reached the crowns of the plants, they may be saved by cutting away all the diseased portions and then grafting the crowns on some healthy stock. Otherwise, it is best to remove the plants at once and burn them. The soil in which they were potted and also the pots, if to be used again, should be sterilized, so that other plants may not be infected from them.

Another disease more common to species of Mamillaria and to a less extent found on Echinocactus and Cereus makes its first appearance as a small, light orange-colored spot on any portion of the plant surface, usually starting at a pulvinus, which seems to be the point at which the infecting germ enters. This spot steadily grows until the plant is totally destroyed. The disease travels inward, toward the center of the plant, following fibrovascular bundles. The colored tissue readily separates from the healthier portion of the plant and is easily removed, but this merely checks its ravages for a time. The disease penetrates every portion of the plant and in time will make itself manifest again in other orange-colored spots on the surface. It is a contagious disease, and the only hope for saving a collection of plants is to destroy all the infected individuals, preferably by burning them. Many remedies for this disease have been applied, but without success.

INSECT PESTS.

The Bureau of Entomology of this Department has investigated cactus insects extensively. The results of this work appear in a bulletin of that Bureau (No. 113), which may be had upon application.

ECONOMIC VALUE OF CACTI.

MEDICINES.

To a limited extent *Cereus grandiflorus* and *C. nycticalus* have been used in the preparation of certain compounds. Other cacti are known to contain characteristic alkaloids which from their peculiar action on the human system may yet prove of value in treating special disorders. Most notable of these forms is the so-called piote bean or mescal button, also known as the dumpling cactus (*Lophophora williamsii* and *L. lewinii*). Since remote times the aborigines of America have used this plant in certain of their religious rites. When the plants are eaten raw, dried or fresh, with water, the optic nerve is so affected that by closing the eyes the user is made to see visions illuminated in the brightest of colors. An alkaloid of this plant has been separated from it and found to contain the same properties. It is not impossible that in time it may be found of value in the treatment of certain ocular disorders. However, no member of the family seems as yet to have yielded a drug that has been used to any considerable extent as a medicine.

GARDEN VEGETABLE.

Among the poorer classes of Mexico the very tender growths of Opuntia are eaten raw, made into a sort of salad, or are cooked, as may be desired. There is little to commend this cactus to those having access to the common and more palatable vegetables of the garden.

FRUITS.

The fruits of a great many species of cacti are very agreeable to the taste, as well as refreshing and nourishing. This is especially true of many species of Opuntia known as tunas. (Pls. IV and V.) In certain parts of Mexico the tuna forms a considerable part of the diet of the poorer natives. In many places it is grown for the market and finds ready sale among all classes. The outer part is peeled away in the same manner as in paring an apple or peach for consumption raw. The inner pulp, containing the seeds, not only possesses a pleasant flavor, but it also creates the impression of being cool even in the hottest weather. Forms of tuna have as wide a range in color, flavor, and size as many of our northern fruits.

Numerous smaller fruits are gathered from wild plants, either for home consumption or for sale in the market. Among these may be mentioned the small, globose, red fruit of *Cereus geometrizans* and kindred species, which is very sweet. It is called "garambullo" by the Mexicans. A number of species of Mamillaria produce an abundance of smaller club-shaped red fruits which have a very pleasant, sweet taste, combined with a slightly acid tang, and are eaten by the natives, who call them "chilitos." The above-mentioned fruits, and also that of *Cereus giganteus*, are quite commonly used in the preparation of preserves, jams, and cakes of somewhat jellylike consistency. These preparations represent some of the choice delicacies of the natives and are to be found on sale in the markets and on the streets of Mexican cities. The fleshy interior of certain species of Echinocactus is used in the production of the so-called cactus candy. The flesh is cut into layers and cured in sugar sirup and allowed to dry, similar to the manner in which citron is prepared for market. The cactus flesh merely forms a foundation, adding perhaps a little flavor.

WOOD.

For the most part all cactus plants are composed of soft, water-laden tissue, but the axis of the plant is composed of a woody core, which in some species makes a considerable development, especially in Opuntia and the large species of Cereus. This woody portion is always more or less porous and usually of an open, lacelike structure, so that it is of little value as compared with other woods. Nevertheless, it is used to some extent in the manufacture of ornaments and rustic work, but more for its curious structure than for any real value the wood may possess. Some of the cylindrical forms of Opuntia yield rather grotesque and ornamental walking canes, as do also a few of the slender-growing columnar species of Cereus. These forms also furnish wood for rustic picture frames, ornamental pincushions, trays, inkwell stands, and the like. To a limited extent the wood of the taller growing species forms material in the shape of poles for the construction of fences and temporary huts.

HEDGES.

Because of their animal-resisting armor of spines, combined with their habit of growth, certain species of cacti are naturally adapted for use as efficient hedge plants wherever they grow in the open throughout the year. The one species most commonly used in Mexico for this purpose is the organo (*Cereus marginatus*), Pl. VI, so called because of its fancied resemblance to the pipe of an organ. It branches freely from the base near the surface of the ground, and these branches immediately assume an upright habit of growth. Growing closely together they soon produce an impenetrable barrier. Its habits of growth recommend it, since there are scarcely any branches above the base and these never spread and cover any great area, thus making a compact, dense, and comparatively narrow hedge. *Cereus stellatus* and *C. weberi* are also used in the regions where they are abundant as native plants, but they have the disadvantage of making a thicker and more open hedge and consequently cover more ground. Where narrowness of the hedge is of minor importance, many of the taller growing species of Opuntia make an equally serviceable barrier and are at all times decorative, especially when bearing an abundance of flowers and fruits.

DECORATIVE VALUE OF CACTI.

It is not intended to convey the idea that cacti, as a whole, can hope to rival many other groups of plants in gorgeous display. For the most part they lack the foliage that lends so much to the value of other plants, and in most instances the flowers, when present, are either too small, too few (Pls. VII, VIII, IX, and X), or too short lived to be considered of any great worth. In some of the climbing species of Cereus and in Phyllocactus the flowers attain a very considerable size, and their waxlike texture and pure whiteness or delicately tinted red, pink, or cream colors present a combination that always calls forth exclamations of wonder and pleasant surprise. Many forms bloom at night, and their flowers are always white and to a slight degree pleasantly fragrant. The flowers are usually produced in periods, each period lasting from one to three or four days. At such a period the plants, if mature and vigorous, will bear a large number of flower buds, which open in the evening after sunset and close with the approach of strong morning light, never again to open. The following night other buds will bloom, and so on until in a few days all will have passed the blooming period, which, after an interval of time, will recur. In our northern conservatories there are usually three or four such periods during the summer season, averaging about four or five weeks apart. On these occasions the display of large white flowers in abundance in the moonlight is a wonderful sight. Most of the species of Echinocereus produce comparatively large showy flowers in a crown about the ends of the branches. They are very attractive in their highly colored (yellow, orange, red, and purple) waxy flowers, but they do not respond so readily to cultivation as many others, especially in greenhouses. Some species of Echinopsis also produce flowers in abundance for a period of a few days. These are trumpet shaped, upright, about 8 inches long, forming a crown about the top of the plant. They range in color from pure white to pale yellow or rosy pink.

The chief attractiveness and beauty in cacti as a group[1] is the remarkable symmetry of growth in the individual plants. The columnar, and most of the genera of smaller cylindrical or globular forms, have clean-cut, longitudinal, parallel angles, ribs, or wings, and located on them at regular intervals are the buds, or pulvini, which bear the spines and flowers, and from which side branches may be developed. The coloring of the epidermis of the plant is frequently very attractive. While in most species this color is some shade of green, many specimens are coated over to a greater or lesser extent with white or bluish glaucousness. In some species the surface is dotted over with very small bunches of velvety white hair, as in *Echinocactus myriostigma*, *E. ornatus*, and *E. capricornus*. Other species are mottled with purple, which in the young growths of *E. ingens* is arranged in transverse bands, alternating with bright green. The coloring of the spines, too, is often exceedingly attractive, especially in the younger growths. It ranges from pure white to amber, yellow, red, and black. Frequently some of these colors are combined on one spine in either longitudinal stripes or transverse bands, and the perfectly uniform variegation is very striking. The form, structure, and arrangement of the spines are in most instances remarkable and show a wonderful adherence to a definite plan of symmetrical arrangement. In certain species some of the spines have a structure of soft and hard transverse layers from base to tip, giving an uneven though uniformly wavy surface much like that of a goat's horn. The larger number of spines are straight or only slightly curved; others have the end curved in the form of a fishhook. Nearly all of them are rather stiff, but some are soft and featherlike

---

[1] See Safford, W. E., "Cactaceæ of Northeastern and Central Mexico, Together with a Synopsis of the Principal Mexican Genera," in Annual Report, Smithsonian Institution, 1908, pp. 525-563, in which are illustrations of many species of Cactaceæ.

in structure and others are thin, flat, paperlike, and flexible. Again, in some species the spines are entirely absent. Mamillaria (Pls. I and II) and some groups of Echinocactus have all the variations of characters already described, but differ materially in body structure. In them the ribs or angles have entirely disappeared and are represented by rows of tubercles or mammæ, each bearing at its summit a cluster of spines. In this group the tubercles are not arranged in longitudinal rows, but are geometrically tesselated over the plant surface, so arranged as to form spirals running in both directions about the plant.

A remarkable and interesting feature is the regularity in number with which these spiral rows appear. As a rule they fall into the numbers 5, 8, 13, 21, 34, 55, and possibly higher numbers. For instance, if it is found that there are 13 parallel rows of tubercles running obliquely around the plant in one direction, there will be either 8 or 21 such parallel rows running obliquely around it in the other direction. Whatever the number of rows counted in one direction, the number counted in the opposite direction will be the one either preceding or following it in the series. Exceptions to this rule are rare, and when one is noted the numbers are usually found to be the doubles of two adjacent numbers in the above series, as 10, 16, 26, 42, and so on. Another interesting fact is that each number in the series is the sum of the two immediately preceding it.

Symmetry is the greatest attraction in this group of plants. Monstrosities are, however, not infrequent in the family, usually assuming a cristate or cockscomb form of growth. These forms are so odd in appearance that they are frequently sought after, and it is not uncommon to find them represented in the collections of amateurs. Their very grotesqueness commends them to the consideration of collectors.

SINGLE PLANT DISPLAYS.

Each individual plant has an attraction of its own. (Pls. XI, XII, and XIII.) Whether it be the symmetrical order of its trunk, its color, its versicolored or versiform spines, or a combination of all these features, supplemented in its proper seasons by the production of flowers and fruits, each normal, healthy plant is well worthy of consideration as an individual specimen. Their adaptability is such as to commend them for situations where many other plants could not exist. They do not require frequent repotting and replenishing of soil, and subsist best on a minimum of water, so that if necessarily neglected for a time they do not materially suffer. A single plant is well worth the little trouble required for its keeping. It occupies a very small amount of space in comparison to its weight, which is an advantage in many instances.

A pretty and interesting display may be had by arranging the plants in groups on benches, on window sills, or on bracket shelves on either side of a window. Pots of individual plants of various sizes lend themselves very readily to artistic arrangement. In any banking effect the larger and taller ones should be placed in the background, and the rest graded down to the front according to the size of the plants. Should the plants be too uniform in size for such arrangement, those in the background may be elevated on inverted pots or blocks of wood of suitable height.

GROUPINGS.

Pleasing effects may be obtained by placing a number of plants in one pot or small box. For this purpose it is necessary to choose small plants, preferably the low-growing globular or short, cylindrical forms of Mamillaria and Echinocactus. With a little care in the selection of perfectly symmetrical plants with well-developed spines, and some taste in arrangement, a compact group may be built up which will make an excellent ornament for the table or window and can easily be moved to any place desired. In the diversity of designs which may be followed there is a wide range of possibilities, ornamental pots or boxes lending an artistic touch to the composition.

PLANTINGS IN OPEN GROUND.

Cactus roots naturally penetrate deep into the soil, and at the same time some of them spread widely from the plant stem. This tendency is necessarily limited in potted plants, and the plant does not receive the nourishment or water that it should have; hence it is always better to place them in the open ground if possible. In the Northern States it is necessary that the plants be protected from frost in winter. In such localities a room in a greenhouse may be set aside for this group of plants, and beds made in the native earth to receive them. Here they may be placed close together, as they shade one another very little and do not have the abundant foliage of other plants. The roots may intermingle, but to no greatly detrimental extent, since the main feeding roots penetrate deep down into the soil. Furthermore, cactus plants need comparatively little nourishment, and it would require a long period of time to exhaust the soil. An effective arrangement is to build up rocks and soil, leaving the surface more or less covered with rocks, making a genuine rockery. (Pl. XVII.) This treatment lends a natural aspect to the surroundings and furthermore adds a greater degree of drainage, so necessary to cacti at all times.

Cacti may be used as good decorative plants in outdoor beds, planted either temporarily or permanently. (Pl. XVI.) Where one has a number of individual potted plants that have to be housed for protection in the winter season, it is always desirable that they be placed in the open during the summer months. They should be taken out as soon as all danger from frost is past and left till danger from frost threatens in the fall. The beds should be either high or on a sloping surface, to insure thorough drainage about the plants. With such plants it is better to leave them potted and plunge the pots into the soil. (Pls. XIV and XV.) Plants thus exposed to the sunshine and rain during the summer months will do far better than those kept indoors and given house treatment. A judicious arranging of the plants in such beds will have an attractive and pleasing effect. Where a large number of individuals of a few species are available, some artistic designs may be worked out in these summer beds.

In the warmer southern or southwestern portions of our country a very large number of cacti will thrive out of doors the year round. In such localities the possibilities for bed planting have a much wider range. More area may be given to them there than would be necessary in the conservatories of the North. They will require greater space, because plants that grow in the open thrive much better than potted ones and consequently branch and spread over a greater area. In such localities, with plenty of room, it is possible to produce decidedly realistic landscape effects. Especially is this true in parks (Pls. XVI and XVII), where the semiarid character of the native home of the cacti may be reproduced with wonderful accuracy. Winding paths may be laid out through the tract and the borders planted in irregular groups, so that the effect will change as one passes along any of the walks.

CULTIVATED FORMS OF CACTI.

The following list contains the names of most of the cacti now in cultivation in the United States. Many other forms are to be found in collections but are not at all common. They are grouped with reference to their habits of growth. Measurements, where given, refer to mature plants and are only approximate. The list, arranged as it is with reference to size, will serve as a guide to prospective purchasers in dealing with collectors and traders.

COLUMNAR FORMS OF CACTI.

Tall—over 6 feet in height.

Cephalocereus:	Cereus—Contd.	Cereus—Contd.	Pilocereus—Contd.
chrysomalus.	euphorbioides.	peruvianus.	cometes.
senilis.	forbesii.	pringlei.	exerens.
Cereus:	geometrizans.	serpentinus.	fulviceps.
azureus.	giganteus.	stellatus.	hoppenstedtii.
baumannii.	hankeanus.	thurberi.	houlletii.
chiotilla.	hildmannianus.	weberi.	lanuginosus.
coerulescens.	jamacaru.	Opuntia:	polylophus.
columnaris.	macrogonus.	cereiformis.	russelianus.
dumortieri.	marginatus.	Pilocereus:	schottii.
eburneus.	pecten-aboriginum.	chrysacanthus.	strictus.

COLUMNAR FORMS OF CACTI—Continued.

Lower—from 1 to 6 feet in height.

Cereus:	Cereus—Contd.	Echinocactus:	Echinocactus—Contd.
candicans.	spachianus.	cylindraceus.	pilosus.
emoryi.	speciosus.	ingens. (Pl. XVIII.)	recurvus.
eruca.	thelegonus.	johnsonii.	Echinopsis:
gummosus.		ornatus.	eyriesii.
mamillatus.		peninsulae.	

Short—less than 1 foot in height.

Echinocactus:	Echinocereus:	Echinocereus—Contd.	Mamillaria—Contd.
anfractuosus.	acifer.	phoeniceus.	erecta.
beguinii.	berlandieri.	procumbens.	eriacantha.
bicolor.	chloranthus.	rigidissimus.	grahamii.
capricornus.	cinerascens.	roemeri.	gracilis.
gibbosus.	conglomeratus.	stramineus.	halei.
intertextus.	ctenoides.	viridiflorus.	leona.
krausei.	dasyacanthus.	Mamillaria:	macromeris.
lenninghauseii.	dubius.	carnea.	microthele.
leucacanthus.	engelmannii.	clava.	radiosa.
longihamatus.	fendleri.	conoidea.	raphidacantha.
scheeri.	knippelianus.	cornifera.	roseana.
uncinatus.	mojavensis.	dolichocentra.	setispina.
whipplei.	paucispinus.	elegans.	spinosissima.
	pectinatus.	elongata.	strobiliformis.

GLOBOSE FORMS OF CACTI.

Large—more than 1 foot in diameter.

Echinocactus:	Echinocactus—Contd.	Echinocactus—Contd.	Echinocactus—Contd.
electracanthus.	grusonii.	longihamatus.	wislizeni.
emoryi.	ingens.		

Medium—from 3 inches to 1 foot in diameter.

Ariocarpus:	Echinocactus—Contd.	Echinopsis:	Mamillaria—Contd.
fissuratus.	horizonthalonius.	gemmata.	melanocentra.
retusus.	lophothele.	multiplex.	mutabilis.
Echinocactus:	multicostatus.	nigricans.	radiosa.
albatus.	myriostigma.	oxygona.	robustispina.
capricornus.	polycephalus.	Leuchtenbergia:	scheeri.
coptonogonus.	robustus.	principis.	seitziana.
corniger.	setispinus.	Mamillaria:	Melocactus:
crispatus.	texensis.	celsiana.	communis.
heterochromus.	unguispinus.	gigantea.	ferox.
hexaedrophorus.		heeseana.	

Small—less than 3 inches in diameter.

Ariocarpus:	Lophophora:	Mamillaria—Contd.	Mamillaria—Contd.
kotschubeyanus.	lewinii.	formosa.	pusilla.
Echinocactus:	williamsii.	gummifera.	radians.
denudatus.	Mamillaria:	heyderi.	recurvata.
humilis.	angularis.	lasiacantha.	rhodantha.
intertextus.	bicolor.	lesaunieri.	schelhasei.
macdowellii.	bocasana.	longimamma.	sempervivi.
mammulosus.	candida.	meiacantha.	senilis.
minusculus.	caput-medusae.	micromeris.	sphaerica.
ottonis.	carretii.	missouriensis.	uncinata.
schickendantzii.	centricirrha.	parkinsonii.	wildii.
schilinzkyanus.	decipiens.	perbella.	zephyranthoides.
simpsoni.	dioica.	phellosperma.	Pelecyphora:
submammulosus.	elegans.	plumosa.	aselliformis.
tabularis.	elephantidens.	polyedra.	pectinata.
turbiniformis.			

PLATYOPUNTIAS AND NOPALEAS.

Tall forms—over 6 feet in height.

Opuntia:
  brasiliensis.
  chlorotricha.
  engelmannii.

Opuntia—Contd.
  ficus indica.
  leucotricha.
  puberula.

Opuntia—Contd.
  robusta.
  tomentosa.
  tuna.

Nopalea:
  auberi.
  dejecta.

Medium forms—2 to 6 feet in height.

Opuntia:
  camanchica.
  curassavica.

Opuntia—Contd.
  microdasys.
  monacantha.

Opuntia—Contd.
  monacantha variegata.
  rafinesquei.

Nopalea:
  coccinellifera.

Low or decumbent forms—less than 2 feet in height.

Opuntia:
  arenaria.
  basilaris.
  decumbens.

Opuntia—Contd.
  fragilis.
  missouriensis.
  pes-corvi.

Opuntia—Contd.
  procumbens.
  rutila.
  strigilis.

Opuntia—Contd.
  ursina.
  vulgaris.

CYLINDROPUNTIAS.

Tall forms—over 6 feet in height.

Opuntia:
  acanthocarpa.
  arbuscula.

Opuntia—Contd.
  bigelowii.
  fulgida.

Opuntia—Contd.
  imbricata.

Opuntia—Contd.
  prolifera.

Medium forms—1 to 6 feet in height.

Opuntia:
  alcahes.
  bernardina.
  cholla.

Opuntia—Contd.
  echinocarpa.
  leptocaulis.

Opuntia—Contd.
  salmiana.
  subulata.

Opuntia—Contd.
  versicolor.
  whipplei.

Low or prostrate forms—less than 1 foot in height.

Opuntia:
  clava.
  davisii.

Opuntia—Contd.
  diademata.
  emoryi.

Opuntia—Contd.
  grahamii.
  parryi.

Opuntia—Contd.
  schottii.

FOLIAGE-BEARING CACTI.

Climbing or clambering forms.

Peireskia:
  aculeata.
  godseffiana.

Peireskiopsis:
  brandegeei.
  spathulata.

Shrubs or small trees.

Peireskia:
  amapola.
  bleo.

Peireskia—Contd.
  nicoyana.

CLIMBING, NIGHT-BLOOMING FORMS OF CEREUS.

Cereus:
  baxaniensis.
  bonplandii.
  grandiflorus.
  hamatus.

Cereus—Contd.
  irradians.
  macdonaldiae.
  martini.

Cereus—Contd.
  nycticalus.
  ocamponis.
  setaceus.

Cereus—Contd.
  spinulosus.
  tortuosus.
  triangularis.

PLANTS NATIVE TO MOIST TROPICAL REGIONS.

Terrestrial.

Phyllocactus:
  ackermannii.
  acuminatus.
  anguliger.

Phyllocactus—Contd.
  crenatus.
  grandis.

Phyllocactus—Contd.
  hookeri.
  phyllanthoides.

Phyllocactus—Contd.
  stenopetalus.
  strictus.

Epiphytic.

Cereus:
  flagelliformis.
Epiphyllum:
  gaertneri.
  russellianum.
  truncatum.

Hariota:
  salicornioides.
Rhipsalis:
  anceps.
  cassytha.

Rhipsalis—Contd.
  conferta.
  grandiflora.
  houllitiana.
  mesembryanthemoides.

Rhipsalis—Contd.
  paradoxa.
  pentaptera.
  rhombea.
  saglionis.

ECHINOCACTUS INGENS, SHOWING THE ZEBRALIKE MARKINGS OF YOUNG OFFSHOOTS, TEHUACAN, MEXICO, 1905.

(Photographed by Trelease.)

Succulent Rockery in Alamo Park, San Antonio, Tex., 1904.

(Photographed by Griffiths.)

CACTUS GARDEN, A. S. WHITE PARK, RIVERSIDE, CAL., 1905.

(Photographed by Griffith.)

Mamillarias Planted in Formal Design, Missouri Botanical Garden, St. Louis, 1905.

ORNAMENTAL PLANTING OF CACTI, MISSOURI BOTANICAL GARDEN, ST. LOUIS, 1905.

(Photographed by Griffiths.)

Fig. 2.—Cereus Eburneus, Tomellin, Mexico, 1910.

Fig. 1.—Pilocereus Fulviceps, Tehuacan, Mexico, 1910.

CEREUS STELLATUS (IN FOREGROUND), NATURAL LANDSCAPE AT TOMELLIN, MEXICO, 1909.

(Photographed by Griffiths.)

CEREUS WEBERI PREDOMINATING IN NATURAL LANDSCAPE AT TOMELLIN, MEXICO, 1909.

(Photographed by Griffiths.)

ECHINOPSIS GEMMATA, MISSOURI BOTANICAL GARDEN, ST. LOUIS, 1898.

CEREUS EBURNEUS, MISSOURI BOTANICAL GARDEN, ST. LOUIS, 1905.

MAMILLARIA CORNIFERA, MISSOURI BOTANICAL GARDEN, ST. LOUIS, 1899.